CARYL CHURCHILL

Caryl Churchill has written for the stage, television and radio. Her stage plays include *Owners* (Royal Court Theatre Upstairs, 1972); *Objections to Sex and Violence* (Royal Court, 1975); *Light Shining in Buckinghamshire* (Joint Stock on tour incl. Theatre Upstairs, 1976); *Vinegar Tom* (Monstrous Regiment on tour, incl. Half Moon and ICA, 1976); *Traps* (Theatre Upstairs, 1977), *Cloud Nine* (Joint Stock on tour incl. Royal Court, London, 1979, then Theatre de Lys, New York, 1981); *Three More Sleepless Nights* (Soho Poly and Theatre Upstairs, 1980); *Top Girls* (Royal Court, London, then Public Theatre, New York, 1982); *Fen* (Joint Stock on tour, incl. Almeida and Royal Court, London, then Public Theatre, New York, 1983); *Softcops* (RSC at the Pit, 1984); *A Mouthful of Birds* with David Lan (Joint Stock on tour, incl. Royal Court, 1986); *Serious Money* (Royal Court and Wyndham's, London, then Public Theatre, New York, 1987); *Icecream* (Royal Court, 1989); *Mad Forest* (Central School of Speech and Drama, then Royal Court, 1990); *Lives of the Great Poisoners* with Orlando Gough and Ian Spink (Second Stride on tour, incl. Riverside Studios, London, 1991); *The Skriker* (Royal National Theatre, 1994); *Thyestes* translated from Seneca (Royal Court Theatre Upstairs, 1994); *Hotel* with Orlando Gough and Ian Spink (Second Stride on tour, incl. The Place, London, 1997); *This is a Chair* (London International Festival of Theatre at the Royal Court, 1997); *Blue Heart* (Joint Stock on tour, incl. Royal Court Theatre, 1997) .

Other works by the same author in the same series

Light Shining in Buckinghamshire (TCG)
Traps
Cloud Nine (TCG)
Icecream
Mad Forest (TCG)
The Skriker (TCG)
Thyestes (translated from Seneca)

Collections

Shorts
- *Lovesick*
- *Abortive*
- *Not Not Not Not Not Enough Oxygen*
- *Schreber's Nervous Illness*
- *The Hospital at the Time of the Revolution*
- *The Judge's Wife*
- *The After-Dinner Joke*
- *Seagulls*
- *Three More Sleepless Nights*
- *Hot Fudge*

Plays: Three
- *A Mouthful of Birds* (co-author: David Lan)
- *Icecream*
- *Mad Forest*
- *Lives of the Great Poisoners* (co-authors Orlando Gough and Ian Spink)
- *The Skriker*
- *Thyestes* (translated from Seneca)

CARYL CHURCHILL

Blue Heart

THEATRE
COMMUNICATIONS
GROUP
New York

Blue Heart is published by Theatre Communications Group, Inc.,
355 Lexington Avenue, New York, NY 10017,
by special arrangement with Nick Hern Books Limited

Cover design from an image by Iain Lanyon

A CIP catalogue record for this book is available from
the Library of Congress

ISBN 155936-154-9

First TCG Edition, April 1998
Reprinted 2002, 2004

Blue Heart was first produced by Out of Joint and the Royal Court Theatre at the Theatre Royal, Bury St Edmunds on 14 August 1997. It was first performed at the Traverse Theatre, Edinburgh on 19 August 1997 and opened at the Royal Court Theatre, London on 17 September 1997. The cast was as follows:

Heart's Desire	**Blue Kettle**	
	MOTHER	Gabrielle Blunt
SUZY	ENID	Jacqueline Defferary
YOUNG WOMAN		Karina Fernandez
BRIAN	MR VANE	Bernard Gallagher
ALICE	MRS PLANT	Valerie Lilley
MAISIE	MRS OLIVER	Mary Macleod
	MRS VANE	Eve Pearce
LEWIS	DEREK	Jason Watkins
	MISS CLARENCE	Anna Wing
CHILDREN		Played by children from local groups and schools

Directed by Max Stafford-Clark
Designed by Julian McGowan
Lighting Designer Johanna Town
Sound Designer Paul Arditti

BLUE HEART

HEART'S DESIRE

Characters

BRIAN

ALICE

MAISIE

SUSY

LEWIS

LOTS OF CHILDREN

TWO GUNMEN

YOUNG AUSTRALIAN WOMAN

OFFICIAL

BIRD

Brian and Alice are married. Maisie is Brian's sister. They are all about 60. Susy, their daughter, is 35, Lewis, their son, is younger.

The scene is Brian and Alice's kitchen.

ALICE and MAISIE. ALICE setting knives and forks on table, MAISIE fidgets about the room. BRIAN enters putting on a red sweater.

BRIAN She's taking her time.

ALICE Not really.

They all stop, BRIAN goes out. Others reset to beginning and do exactly what they did before as BRIAN enters putting on a tweed jacket.

BRIAN She's taking her time.

ALICE Not really.

They all stop, BRIAN goes out, others reset and BRIAN enters putting on an old cardigan.

BRIAN She's taking her time.

ALICE Not really.

BRIAN We should have met the plane.

ALICE We should not.

MAISIE What I really envy her for is the fauna because it's down a completely separate branch of evolution and I would love I would really love to see a platypus, not in a zoo but in its natural habitat. Imagine going to feed the ducks and there is something that is not a duck and nor is it a waterrat or a mole, it's the paws make me think of a mole, but imagine this furry creature with its ducky face, it makes you think what else could have existed, tigers with trunks, anyway the platypus has always been my favourite animal, it doesn't lay eggs like a duck, it's a marsupial like a kangaroo so the baby's born like a thread like a speck and has to crawl into the pouch, is that right, is a platypus a marsupial or not actually I'm not sure about that, maybe it does lay eggs like a duck, I'll look it up or I'll ask her when she comes and I wonder if she's ever seen one, maybe she went swimming in a river and there was this little furry –

Reset to top. BRIAN *comes in putting on old cardigan.*

BRIAN She's taking her time.

ALICE Not really.

BRIAN We should have met the plane.

ALICE We should not.

BRIAN She'll be exhausted.

ALICE She's a woman of thirtyfive.

BRIAN How can you speak of your daughter?

ALICE She's a woman of thirtyfive.

BRIAN You're so right of course.

ALICE She can travel round the world, she can travel the last few miles.

BRIAN It's so delightful for you always being so right.

ALICE That's it.

BRIAN It's what?

ALICE I'm leaving.

BRIAN Oh ha ha we're all supposed to be frantic and beg you to stay and say very sorry.

ALICE I wouldn't bother.

BRIAN I'm not going to bother don't worry.

Exit ALICE.

MAISIE Alice?

BRIAN *and* MAISIE *wait.*

BRIAN She'll just have a cry.

ALICE *enters in coat with bag.*

ALICE Tell her I'm sorry and I'll phone later to tell her where I am.

Exit ALICE.

BRIAN Was that the front door? Alice? Alice.

MAISIE I don't think you –

Reset to top, ALICE *in room as before,* MAISIE *as before,* BRIAN *enters putting on old cardigan.*

BRIAN She's taking her time.

ALICE Not really.

BRIAN We should have met the plane.

ALICE We should not.

BRIAN She'll be exhausted.

ALICE She's a woman of thirtyfive.

BRIAN How can you speak of your daughter?

ALICE She's a woman of thirtyfive.

BRIAN You're so right of course.

ALICE — She can travel round the world, she can travel the last few miles.

BRIAN — It's so delightful for you always being so right.

ALICE — She didn't want to be met.

MAISIE — She'll be here in a few minutes.

BRIAN — I'm talking about spontaneity

ALICE — She doesn't want fuss.

BRIAN — She says that but it wouldn't be if she didn't know she was being met and there we just were or there I was –

Phone rings.

Hello? speaking. Ah. Right. Yes. Thank you.

MAISIE — What?

BRIAN — There's been an accident.

ALICE — The plane?

BRIAN — The tube. Didn't I say we should have met her?

ALICE — Is she – ?

Set back to top as before. BRIAN *enters putting on old cardigan.*

BRIAN — She's taking her time.

ALICE — Not really.

BRIAN — We should have met the plane.

ALICE — We should not.

BRIAN — She'll be exhausted.

ALICE She's a woman of thirtyfive.

BRIAN How can you speak of your daughter?

ALICE She's a woman of thirtyfive.

BRIAN You're so right of course.

ALICE She can travel round the world, she can travel the last few miles.

BRIAN It's so delightful for you always being so right.

ALICE She didn't want to be met.

MAISIE She'll be here in a few minutes.

BRIAN I'm talking about spontaneity

ALICE She doesn't want fuss.

BRIAN She says that but it wouldn't be if she didn't know she was being met and there we just were or there I was if you insisted on not coming, she'd like it when it happened, the moment she caught sight she'd be delighted.

ALICE Well we didn't so I don't see the point of worrying about it now.

BRIAN She'll never come home from Australia again.

ALICE What do you mean?

MAISIE *trips over.*

ALICE Oh, what?

BRIAN What the hell?

MAISIE Sorry, all right, I'm all right.

ALICE You haven't hurt yourself?

MAISIE — No. Yes. Not really.

ALICE — Can you get up?

MAISIE — Yes of course. Well. It's just my ankle. Oh dear.

BRIAN — How did you do that?

ALICE — Sit down and let's have a look at it.

MAISIE — Oh ow. No no it's nothing. Ow.

Set back. BRIAN *enters putting on cardigan.*

BRIAN — She's taking her time.

ALICE — Not really.

BRIAN — We should have met the plane.

ALICE — We should not.

BRIAN — She'll be exhausted.

ALICE — She's a woman of thirtyfive.

BRIAN — How can you speak of your daughter.

ALICE — She's a woman of thirtyfive.

BRIAN — You're so right of course.

ALICE — She can travel round the world, she can travel the last few miles.

BRIAN — It's so delightful for you always being so right.

ALICE — She didn't want to be met.

MAISIE — She'll be here in a few minutes.

BRIAN — I'm talking about spontaneity.

ALICE — She doesn't want fuss.

BRIAN She says that but it wouldn't be if she didn't know she was being met and there we just were or there I was if you insisted on not coming, she'd like it when it happened, the moment she caught sight she'd be delighted.

ALICE Well we didn't so I don't see the point of worrying about it now.

BRIAN She'll never come home from Australia again.

ALICE What do you mean? of course she'll come again.

BRIAN In the event she goes back of course she'll come again but she'll never come back for the first time again.

Enter LEWIS, *drunk.*

LEWIS Where is she?

BRIAN You're not coming in here in that condition.

LEWIS Where's my big sister? I want to give her a kiss.

BRIAN You'll see her when you're sober.

ALICE Now it's all right, Brian. Susy isn't here yet, Lewis.

LEWIS You've probably got her hidden under the table. Dad knows where she is, don't you Dad? Daddy always knows where Susy is. Hello Aunty Maisie, want a drink? Let's go to the pub, Maisie, and get away from this load of –

LEWIS *goes, setback as before. This time do the repeat at double speed, all movements accurate though fast.*

BRIAN She's taking her time.

ALICE Not really.

BRIAN We should have met the plane.

ALICE We should not.

BRIAN She'll be exhausted.

ALICE She's a woman of thirtyfive.

BRIAN How can you speak of your daughter?

ALICE She's a woman of thirtyfive.

BRIAN You're so right of course.

ALICE She can travel round the world, she can travel the last few miles.

BRIAN It's so delightful for you always being so right.

ALICE She didn't want to be met.

MAISIE She'll be here in a few minutes.

BRIAN I'm talking about spontaneity.

ALICE She doesn't want fuss.

BRIAN She says that but it wouldn't be if she didn't know she was being met and there we just were or there I was if you insisted on not coming, she'd like it when it happened, the moment she caught sight she'd be delighted.

ALICE Well we didn't so I don't see the point of worrying about it now.

BRIAN She'll never come home from Australia again.

ALICE What do you mean? of course she'll come again.

BRIAN In the event she goes back of course she'll come again but she'll never come back for the first time again.

Resume normal speed.

MAISIE It's all this waiting.

ALICE I hope she does come soon because I'm getting hungry.

BRIAN You don't have to wait to eat.

ALICE No it's her special lunch.

MAISIE Are you going to tell her straight away?

BRIAN That's not something for you to worry about, Maisie.

ALICE We're all in it together.

MAISIE We've all got perfectly good alibis.

BRIAN But they don't believe alibis any more. It's all forensic, it's all genetic.

ALICE But there can't be any forensic if none of us did anything, I don't know why you have to act like a guilty person when it's nothing to do with any of us except that the body was found in our garden, it was dumped in our garden as everybody knows.

MAISIE I keep telling the police about the postman but they haven't taken it in.

BRIAN I happen to know that a great many people are wrongfully convicted and I don't live in a dream that suggests that terrible things only befall people in newspapers.

MAISIE So I'll just say nothing and leave it to you.

Reset to just after 'all this waiting.'

ALICE I hope she does come soon because I'm getting hungry.

BRIAN You don't have to wait to eat.

ALICE No it's her special lunch.

BRIAN I should just go ahead and eat since you've clearly no sense of occasion anyway. She's not going to care if there's lunch, she'll be exhausted, she'll go to bed.

ALICE That's all right if that's what she wants to do.

BRIAN You make yourself a doormat to that girl, you always did, she won't be grateful for lunch she'll be on a diet.

MAISIE Now the one diet that is a good diet is the Hay diet which is to do with not combining –

Reset to just after 'wants to do.'

BRIAN You make yourself a doormat to that girl, you always did, she won't be grateful for lunch she'll be on a diet.

ALICE Are you pleased she's coming back?

BRIAN What's the matter with you now?

ALICE You don't sleem peased – you don't pleem seased –

Reset to after 'coming back.'

BRIAN What's the matter with you now?

ALICE You don't seem pleased, you seem cross.

MAISIE The tube's very quick, she'll be here in no time I'm sure.

A horde of small children rush in, round the room and out again.

Reset to after 'of course she'll come again.'

BRIAN In the event she goes back of course she'll come again but she'll never come back for the first time again.

MAISIE It's all this waiting.

ALICE I hope she does come soon because I'm getting hungry.

BRIAN You don't have to wait to eat.

ALICE No it's her special lunch.

BRIAN I should just go ahead and eat since you've clearly no sense of occasion anyway. She's not going to care if there's lunch, she'll be exhausted, she'll go to bed.

ALICE That's all right if that's what she wants to do.

BRIAN You make yourself a doormat to that girl, you always did, she won't be grateful for lunch she'll be on a diet.

ALICE Are you pleased she's coming back?

BRIAN What's the matter with you now?

ALICE You don't seem pleased, you seem cross.

MAISIE The tube's very quick, she'll be here in no time I'm sure.

BRIAN You're the thing makes me cross, drive me insane with your wittering.

ALICE This should be a lovely day. You spoil everything.

BRIAN You've done it now, it was a lovely day, you've spoilt it.

Enter LEWIS, *drunk.*

LEWIS I'm unhappy. What are you going to do about it?

ALICE You know you have to help yourself, Lewis.

LEWIS But it never stops.

BRIAN Lewis, I wish you'd died at birth. If I'd known what you'd grow up like I'd have killed either you or myself the day you were born.

LEWIS You see this is where I get it from. Is it any wonder?

Reset to after 'doesn't want fuss'.

BRIAN She says that but it wouldn't be if she didn't know she was being met and there we just were or there I was if you insisted on not coming, she'd like it when it happened, the moment she caught sight she'd be delighted.

ALICE Well we didn't so I don't see the point of worrying about it now.

BRIAN She'll never come home from Australia again.

ALICE What do you mean? of course she'll come again.

BRIAN In the event she goes back of course she'll come again but she'll never come back for the first time again.

MAISIE It's all this waiting.

ALICE I hope she does come soon because I'm getting hungry.

BRIAN You don't have to wait to eat.

ALICE — No it's her special lunch.

BRIAN — I should just go ahead and eat since you've clearly no sense of occasion anyway. She's not going to care if there's lunch, she'll be exhausted, she'll go to bed.

ALICE — That's all right if that's what she wants to do.

BRIAN — You make yourself a doormat to that girl, you always did, she won't be grateful for lunch she'll be on a diet.

ALICE — Are you pleased she's coming back?

BRIAN — What's the matter with you now?

ALICE — You don't seem pleased, you seem cross.

MAISIE — The tube's very quick, she'll be here in no time I'm sure.

BRIAN — You're the thing makes me cross, drive me insane with your wittering.

ALICE — This should be a lovely day. You spoil everything.

BRIAN — You've done it now, it was a lovely day, you've spoilt it.

ALICE — All I'm saying is be nice to her.

BRIAN — Be nice to her?

ALICE — Yes I'm just saying be nice to her.

Two GUNMEN *burst in and kill them all, then leave.*

Reset to top. as far as possible keep the movements that go with the part lines.

BRIAN — She's taking

ALICE	Not
BRIAN	We should have
ALICE	We should not
BRIAN	She'll be
ALICE	She's a woman
BRIAN	How can you speak
ALICE	She's a
BRIAN	You're so
ALICE	She can travel
BRIAN	It's so delightful
ALICE	She didn't want
MAISIE	She'll be here
BRIAN	I'm talking about
ALICE	She doesn't
BRIAN	She says that but
ALICE	Well we didn't
BRIAN	She'll never
ALICE	What do you
BRIAN	In the event
MAISIE	It's all this
ALICE	I hope she
BRIAN	You don't have to
ALICE	No it's .
BRIAN	I should just

ALICE	That's all right if
BRIAN	You make yourself a
ALICE	Are you pleased
BRIAN	What's the matter
ALICE	You don't seem
MAISIE	The tube's very
BRIAN	You're the thing
ALICE	This should be a lovely
BRIAN	You've done it
ALICE	All I'm saying is
BRIAN	Be nice
ALICE	Yes I'm just saying be nice to her.
BRIAN	When am I not nice to her? am I not a good father is that what you're going to say? do you want to say that? say it.
ALICE	I'm just –
BRIAN	Say it say it.
ALICE	Just be nice to her that's all.
BRIAN	Nice.
ALICE	Fine, you're going to be nice that's all I'm saying.
BRIAN	I should leave you. I'm the one should have gone to Australia.
ALICE	I wish you had.
BRIAN	Snipsnap, sharp tongue.

ALICE No I do wish you had. Because I'd have stayed here and been happy. Because I'm afraid I haven't been faithful to you.

BRIAN What are you saying? An affair?

ALICE Fifteen years.

BRIAN Did you know about this, Maisie?

ALICE Don't bring Maisie into it.

BRIAN Don't tell me what not to do. Has everyone been deceiving me?

MAISIE I did know a little bit.

BRIAN Fifteen . . . ? you mean when we were on holiday in Portugal you were already . . . ?

Reset to after 'spoilt it'.

ALICE All I'm saying is be nice to her.

BRIAN Be nice to her?

ALICE Yes I'm just saying be nice to her.

BRIAN When am I not nice to her? am I not a good father is that what you're going to say? do you want to say that? say it.

ALICE I'm just –

BRIAN Say it say it.

ALICE Just be nice to her that's all.

BRIAN Nice.

ALICE Fine, you're going to be nice that's all I'm saying.

BRIAN I should leave you. I'm the one should have gone to Australia.

ALICE — Go back with her I should.

BRIAN — Maybe I'll do that.

ALICE — Though mind you she wouldn't stay in Australia in that case would she? She'd have to move on to New Zealand. Or Hawaii, I think she'd move to Tonga probably.

MAISIE — I do think waiting is one of the hardest things.

BRIAN — Waiting isn't the problem.

MAISIE — Is something else?

BRIAN — Of course not.

ALICE — Something is.

BRIAN — I'm terribly hungry.

MAISIE — We're all getting a bit peckish. Why don't I cut up some little cubes of cheese?

BRIAN — No, I'm hungry – I'll tell you.

ALICE — What?

BRIAN — I'm telling you. I have this terrible urge to eat myself.

ALICE — To bite your skin?

BRIAN — Yes to bite but to eat – never mind.

ALICE — No it's all right, you can tell us.

BRIAN — Starting with my fingernails like this –

MAISIE — Yes you always have bitten your fingernails.

BRIAN — But the whole finger, if I hold it with my other hand it won't happen but what I want to do is chew up my finger, I want my whole hand in my mouth. Don't despise me.

ALICE Of course not, dear. I'm sure plenty of people –

BRIAN My whole arm, swallow it right up to the shoulder, then the other arm gobble gobble up to the shoulder, and big bite left big bite right that's both the shoulders in.

MAISIE Is this something you've always wanted to do or –?

BRIAN And the shoulders bring the rest of my body, eat my heart, eat my lungs, down my ribs I go, munch my belly, crunch my prick, and oh my whole body's in my mouth now so there's just my legs sticking out, I've eaten it all up.

ALICE Have you thought of seeing someone about –

BRIAN Then snap snap up my legs to the knees the calves the ankles just the feet sticking out of my mouth now gollop gollop I've swallowed my feet, there's only my head and my big mouth wants it, my big mouth turns round and ahh there goes my head into my mouth I've swallowed my head I've swallowed my whole self up I'm all mouth can my mouth swallow my mouth yes yes my mouth's taking a big bite ahh.

Reset to after 'Tonga probably'.

MAISIE I do think waiting is one of the hardest things.

(*Sings.*) Oh for the wings for the wings of a dove etc.

Reset to after 'just saying be nice to her'.

BRIAN When am I not nice to her? am I not a good father is that what you're going to say? do you want to say that? say it.

ALICE I'm just –

BRIAN Say it say it.

ALICE Just be nice to her that's all.

BRIAN Nice.

ALICE Fine, you're going to be nice that's all I'm saying.

BRIAN I should leave you. I'm the one should have gone to Australia.

ALICE Go back with her I should.

BRIAN Maybe I'll do that.

ALICE Though mind you she wouldn't stay in Australia in that case would she? She'd have to move on to New Zealand. Or Hawaii, I think she'd move to Tonga probably.

MAISIE I do think waiting is one of the hardest things. Waiting for arrivals and also waiting to say goodbye, that's even worse when you're waiting on a station platform or a quayside or the airport or just at home the day someone's going waiting for the time when they go I think that's far worse than when they've gone though of course when they've gone you think why didn't I make better use of them when they were still there, you can't do right in those situations.

BRIAN It's not that you don't have a sense of occasion. You know exactly what an occasion is and you deliberately set out to ruin it. I've thought for forty years you were a stupid woman, now I know you're simply nasty.

LEWIS *comes in, drunk.*

LEWIS It's time we had it out. It's time we spoke the truth.

MAISIE Lewis, you're always speaking the truth and where does it get you?

LEWIS I want my life to begin.

ALICE Lewis, there is one little rule in this house and what is it? it is that you don't come into this room when you've been drinking. Do we stop you drinking? no because we can't stop you drinking. Do we throw you out in the street? no because for some reason we are too tenderhearted and that is probably wrong of us. But there is one little rule and if you keep breaking it –

BRIAN Out. Out.

LEWIS No more. No more. No more.

BRIAN Out.

Reset to top. This time it is only last words that are said, mark gestures and positions at those points as far as possible.

BRIAN time.

ALICE really.

BRIAN the plane.

ALICE not.

BRIAN exhausted.

ALICE	thirtyfive.
BRIAN	your daughter.
ALICE	thirtyfive.
BRIAN	of course.
ALICE	last few miles
BRIAN	so right.
ALICE	to be met.
MAISIE	few minutes.
BRIAN	spontaneity.
ALICE	fuss.
BRIAN	she'd be delighted.
ALICE	now.
BRIAN	again.
ALICE	again.
BRIAN	again.
MAISIE	waiting.
ALICE	getting hungry.
BRIAN	eat.
ALICE	lunch.
BRIAN	bed.
ALICE	wants to do.
BRIAN	on a diet.
ALICE	coming back?
BRIAN	now?

ALICE cross.

MAISIE in no time I'm sure.

BRIAN insane with your wittering.

ALICE spoil everything.

BRIAN spoilt it.

ALICE nice to her.

BRIAN nice to her?

ALICE nice to her.

BRIAN say it.

ALICE just.

BRIAN say it.

ALICE that's all.

BRIAN Nice.

ALICE all I'm saying.

BRIAN Australia.

ALICE I should.

BRIAN do that.

ALICE Tonga probably.

MAISIE in those situations.

BRIAN nasty.

Doorbell rings.

MAISIE *goes off.* ALICE *and* BRIAN *embrace. Cries of welcome off.*

Enter SUSY *with* MAISIE *behind her.*

SUSY — Mummy. Daddy. How wonderful to be home.

Reset to after 'maybe I'll do that'.

ALICE — Though mind you she wouldn't stay in Australia in that case would she? She'd have to move on to New Zealand. Or Hawaii, I think she'd move to Tonga probably.

MAISIE — I do think waiting is one of the hardest things. Waiting for arrivals and also waiting to say goodbye, that's even worse when you're waiting on a station platform or a quayside or the airport or just at home the day someone's going waiting for the time when they go I think that's far worse than when they've gone though of course when they've gone you think why didn't I make better use of them when they were still there, you can't do right in those situations.

BRIAN — It's not that you don't have a sense of occasion. You know exactly what an occasion is and you deliberately set out to ruin it. I've thought for forty years you were a stupid woman, now I know you're simply nasty.

Doorbell rings.

MAISIE — That'll be her.

BRIAN *goes out.*

MAISIE — We'll see a change in her.

BRIAN *returns followed by a young Australian woman.*

ALICE — Oh.

BRIAN	This is a friend, you said a friend of Susy's, I don't quite . . .
ALICE	Hello do come in. How lovely. Did you travel together?
YW	It's great to be here. Susy's told me so much about you. She said to be sure to look you up.
BRIAN	And she's just behind you is she?
ALICE	Did you travel in separately from the airport? Did you come on the tube?
YW	I came on a bus.
ALICE	That's a good way.
YW	But what's this about Susy? Susy's not here.
MAISIE	She hasn't arrived yet.
YW	Susy's coming too? that's amazing. She saw me off on the plane.
BRIAN	Of course Susy's coming.
MAISIE	Do you know Susy very well? is she an old friend?
YW	I live with Susy. Hasn't she told you about me? I thought she wrote to tell you to expect me.
ALICE	I'm terribly sorry, I don't think . . .
MAISIE	Is Susy not coming home?
YW	I thought that was something she didn't want to do but of course I could be wrong. She said she was coming?
	Reset to after 'those situations'.

BRIAN — It's not that you don't have a sense of occasion. You know exactly what an occasion is and you deliberately set out to ruin it. I've thought for forty years you were a stupid woman, now I know you're simply nasty.

Doorbell rings.

MAISIE — That'll be her.

ALICE — Do you want to go?

BRIAN *goes off and comes back almost at once jostled by a man in uniform.*

OFFICIAL — Papers.

ALICE — What?

BRIAN — Papers, he has to see our papers. Passport. Driving licence. Birth certificate. Season ticket. Our papers are all in order. I'm sure you'll find everything in order.

MAISIE — Don't let them take me away.

Reset to after 'getting hungry', go as fast as possible. Precision matters, intelligibility doesn't.

ALICE — I hope she does come soon because I'm getting hungry.

BRIAN — You don't have to wait to eat.

ALICE — No it's her special lunch.

BRIAN — I should just go ahead and eat since you've clearly no sense of occasion anyway. She's not going to care if there's lunch, she'll be exhausted, she'll go to bed.

ALICE — That's all right if that's what she wants to do.

BRIAN — You make yourself a doormat to that girl, you always did, she won't be grateful for lunch she'll be on a diet.

ALICE — Are you pleased she's coming back?

BRIAN — What's the matter with you now?

ALICE — You don't seem pleased, you seem cross.

MAISIE — The tube's very quick, she'll be here in no time I'm sure.

BRIAN — You're the thing makes me cross, drive me insane with your wittering.

ALICE — This should be a lovely day. You spoil everything.

BRIAN — You've done it now, it was a lovely day, you've spoilt it.

ALICE — All I'm saying is be nice to her.

BRIAN — Be nice to her?

ALICE — Yes I'm just saying be nice to her.

BRIAN — When am I not nice to her? am I not a good father is that what you're going to say? do you want to say that? say it.

ALICE — I'm just –

BRIAN — Say it say it.

ALICE — Just be nice to her that's all.

BRIAN — Nice.

ALICE — Fine, you're going to be nice that's all I'm saying.

BRIAN — I should leave you. I'm the one should have gone to Australia.

ALICE Go back with her I should.

BRIAN Maybe I'll do that.

ALICE Though mind you she wouldn't stay in Australia in that case would she? She'd have to move on to New Zealand. Or Hawaii, I think she'd move to Tonga probably.

MAISIE I do think waiting is one of the hardest things. Waiting for arrivals and also waiting to say goodbye, that's even worse when you're waiting on a station platform or a quayside or the airport or just at home the day someone's going waiting for the time when they go I think that's far worse than when they've gone though of course when they've gone you think why didn't I make better use of them when they were still there, you can't do right on those occasions.

Set back to after 'worse than when they've gone' Continue at speed.

MAISIE though of course when they've gone you think why didn't I make better use of them when they were still there, you can't do right in those situations.

BRIAN It's not that you don't have a sense of occasion. You know exactly what an occasion is and you deliberately set out to ruin it. I've thought for forty years you were a stupid woman, now I know you're simply nasty.

Doorbell rings. Return to normal speed.

MAISIE That'll be her.

ALICE Do you want to go?

BRIAN *goes off. A ten foot tall bird enters.*

Reset to after 'situations'.

BRIAN It's not occasion occasion deliberately ruin it forty years stupid nasty.

Doorbell rings.

MAISIE That'll be her.

ALICE Do you want to go?

Silence. They don't answer the door and they wait in silence a longer time than you think you can get away with.

Reset to after 'nasty'.

Doorbell rings.

MAISIE That'll be her.

ALICE Do you want to go?

BRIAN *doesn't move.* ALICE *goes off.*

MAISIE Do you ever wake up in the night and be frightened of dying? I'm not at all bothered in the daytime. We've all got to do it after all. Think what a lot of people have done it already. Even the young will have to, even the ones who haven't been born yet will have to, it's not a problem theoretically is it, it's the condition of life. I'm not afraid of an afterlife well maybe a little, I'd rather there wasn't one wouldn't you, imagine finding you were dead that would be frightening but of course maybe it wouldn't we don't know, but really I think we just stop, I think either we're alive or we know nothing so death never really happens to us, but still sometimes in the night there's a chill in my blood and I think what is it what am I frightened of and then I think oh death that's what it is again and I –

Reset to after 'that'll be her'.

ALICE Do you want to go?

BRIAN *doesn't move.* ALICE *goes out. Cries of welcome off.* ALICE *and* SUSY *enter.*

SUSY Here I am.

BRIAN You are my heart's desire.

Reset to top. BRIAN *enters putting on cardigan.*

BRIAN She's taking her time.

ALICE Not really.

BRIAN We should have met the plane.

ALICE We should not.

BRIAN She'll be exhausted.

ALICE She's a woman of thirtyfive.

BRIAN How can you speak of your daughter?

ALICE She's a woman of thirtyfive.

BRIAN You're so right of course.

ALICE She can travel round the world, she can travel the last few miles.

BRIAN It's so delightful for you always being so right.

ALICE She didn't want to be met.

MAISIE She'll be here in a few minutes.

BRIAN I'm talking about spontaneity.

ALICE She doesn't want fuss.

BRIAN She says that but it wouldn't be if she didn't know she was being met and there we just were or there I was if you insisted on not coming, she'd like it when it happened, the moment she caught sight she'd be delighted.

ALICE Well we didn't so I don't see the point of worrying about it now.

BRIAN She'll never come home from Australia again.

ALICE What do you mean? of course she'll come again.

BRIAN In the event she goes back of course she'll come again but she'll never come back for the first time again.

MAISIE It's all this waiting.

ALICE I hope she does come soon because I'm getting hungry.

BRIAN You don't have to wait to eat.

ALICE No it's her special lunch.

BRIAN I should just go ahead and eat since you've clearly no sense of occasion anyway. She's not going to care if there's lunch, she'll be exhausted, she'll go to bed.

ALICE That's all right if that's what she wants to do.

BRIAN You make yourself a doormat to that girl, you always did, she won't be grateful for lunch she'll be on a diet.

ALICE Are you pleased she's coming back?

BRIAN What's the matter with you now?

ALICE — You don't seem pleased, you seem cross.

MAISIE — The tube's very quick, she'll be here in no time I'm sure.

BRIAN — You're the thing makes me cross, drive me insane with your wittering.

ALICE — This should be a lovely day. You spoil everything.

BRIAN — You've done it now, it was a lovely day, you've spoilt it.

ALICE — All I'm saying is be nice to her.

BRIAN — Be nice to her?

ALICE — Yes I'm just saying be nice to her.

BRIAN — When am I not nice to her? am I not a good father is that what you're going to say? do you want to say that? say it.

ALICE — I'm just –

BRIAN — Say it say it.

ALICE — Just be nice to her that's all.

BRIAN — Nice.

ALICE — Fine, you're going to be nice that's all I'm saying.

BRIAN — I should leave you. I'm the one should have gone to Australia.

ALICE — Go back with her I should.

BRIAN — Maybe I'll do that.

ALICE — Though mind you she wouldn't stay in Australia in that case would she? She'd have to move on to New Zealand. Or Hawaii, I think she'd move to Tonga probably.

MAISIE — I do think waiting is one of the hardest things. Waiting for arrivals and also waiting to say goodbye, that's even worse when you're waiting on a station platform or a quayside or the airport or just at home the day someone's going waiting for the time when they go I think that's far worse than when they've gone though of course when they've gone you think why didn't I make better use of them when they were still there, you can't do right in those situations.

BRIAN — It's not that you don't have a sense of occasion. You know exactly what an occasion is and you deliberately set out to ruin it. I've thought for forty years you were a stupid woman, now I know you're simply nasty.

Doorbell rings.

MAISIE — That'll be her.

ALICE — Do you want to go?

BRIAN *doesn't move.* ALICE *goes out. Cries of welcome off.* ALICE *and* SUSY *enter.*

SUSY — Here I am.

BRIAN — Here you are.

ALICE — Yes here she is.

SUSY — Hello aunty.

BRIAN — You are my heart's –

Reset to top. BRIAN *enters putting on old cardigan.*

BRIAN — She's taking her time.

End.

BLUE KETTLE

Characters

DEREK, *40*

ENID, *30*

MRS PLANT, *late 50s*

MRS OLIVER, *over 60*

MRS VANE, *mid 70s*

MR VANE, *mid 70s*

MISS CLARENCE, *80*

DEREK'S MOTHER, *70*

Scenes 1, 2, 4, 6, are in public places – cafe, station, park.

Scenes 3, 5, 9, 10, 11, are in Derek and Enid's flat.

Scene 7 is at the Vanes' house.

Scene 8 is in a geriatric ward.

1. DEREK, MRS PLANT.

MRS PLANT I can't speak.

DEREK Don't worry.

MRS PLANT Let me look at you.

DEREK Have I got your nose?

MRS PLANT You might have your father's mouth. I can't quite see his mouth but now I see yours . . .

DEREK My mouth?

MRS PLANT Your grandmother's eyes were that colour. Yes, he had a smile.

DEREK Bit of a heartbreaker was he, my dad? You don't mind me asking?

MRS PLANT Bit of a shit of course but at the time, if I tell you he was twenty-two and I was sixteen. And he had a lambretta. What does that mean, you'll say. I'd hold on round his back and we could get out into the country. I've been in fields since but I've never seen buttercups comparable.

DEREK So you'd say you'd got happy memories?

MRS PLANT I've memories of having been happy certainly but then I saw him in the street with Julia Studley and it was after that I found out what had happened and I told them I'd be ashamed to marry someone that didn't want me and they said all right but it's adoption then. Because you didn't have abortion like now and anyway I was already thinking of it as a little doll. So there's that much to thank me for.

DEREK I do.

MRS PLANT Where do you live?

DEREK In London.

MRS PLANT What part of London?

DEREK Crouch End.

MRS PLANT No I don't know that.

DEREK What's your husband going to say?

MRS PLANT He'll be glad for me.

DEREK Will he?

MRS PLANT He's always known all about it. Your brothers don't know.

DEREK What will they say?

MRS PLANT We'll find out.

DEREK I don't want to embarrass you.

MRS PLANT You couldn't ever embarrass me, my dear. And are you all right where you live?

DEREK I'm fine, yes.

MRS PLANT Do you live on your own?

DEREK I've got a girlfriend.

MRS PLANT That's nice. What's her name?

DEREK Enid.

MRS PLANT That's nice, it's an oldfashioned name.

DEREK — She's called after her grandmother.

MRS PLANT — Do you hate me?

DEREK — No, I think you're wonderful.

MRS PLANT — I had a name for you. I called you Tom. But when I gave you up I said you hadn't got a name, I thought who you went to would like to give you their own name, I thought that was fair.

DEREK — Tom's nice.

MRS PLANT — Do you like it?

DEREK — Yes I do.

2. DEREK, MRS OLIVER.

MRS OLIVER — I brought some photographs. I don't know if you want to see them.

DEREK — I'd love to.

MRS OLIVER — This is my sister Eileen. And here she is again with her husband Bob and the twins. That's thirty years ago. This is my parents. He was a good looking man. This is me and Brian and the girls when they were little and this is Mary grown up and her husband Phil and their two which is Billy and Megan, now you may not agree but I think where the family likeness is is in Billy you see which is your nephew. Do you see what I mean?

DEREK Yes I do.

MRS OLIVER Round the eyes.

DEREK The eyes yes and –

MRS OLIVER Something about the shape of the head I think.

DEREK You're right, yes.

MRS OLIVER And where that comes from is my father and *his* father though I don't have a picture with me of him, he was a cabinet maker in Yorkshire. This is my other daughter you see, Jenny, and hers, which is Kevin, Mat and Susy. Now what you'll want to see, I do have this one picture of your father, it's not very clear but it's better than nothing. He was better looking than that. The sun was in his eyes.

DEREK He looks great.

MRS OLIVER He was all right.

DEREK Do you mind if I ask . . . Does your family know about me?

MRS OLIVER No.

DEREK No they don't know?

MRS OLIVER No.

DEREK They don't know, no. That's understandable.

MRS OLIVER I never told my husband.

DEREK So of course you wouldn't want to now.

MRS OLIVER He's dead now.

DEREK I'm sorry.

MRS OLIVER It makes things easier for you. But I'm not pleased about that. I'd rather have told him. I don't like starting something up now that he never knew about.

DEREK You don't have to blue anything up.

MRS OLIVER I have done. I've come and met you.

DEREK Well it's good we've set eyes on each other. It means a lot to me.

MRS OLIVER I have this entire family.

DEREK I appreciate that.

MRS OLIVER Do your parents, your adoptive parents should I call them, your real parents, do they know you've done this?

DEREK No they don't.

MRS OLIVER And will you tell them?

DEREK They don't know I know I'm adopted. I found out by mistake when I was sixteen and I kept waiting and I never said anything.

MRS OLIVER There you are.

DEREK I'm not saying it's an easy situation.

MRS OLIVER We don't necessarily have anything in common.

DEREK Of course not.

MRS OLIVER Do you believe in heredity?

DEREK A bit.

MRS OLIVER But then there's how you're brought up. There's family jokes.

DEREK Exactly.

MRS OLIVER I mean I look at you and you could be anyone.

DEREK Of course.

MRS OLIVER You shouldn't expect to be loved.

DEREK I don't.

MRS OLIVER You have been loved I hope? by your family?

DEREK Yes I have.

MRS OLIVER That's a relief anyway.

DEREK We don't have to see each other again.

MRS OLIVER Of course we don't have to.

DEREK We have the choice. And we don't have to make a choice. The choice is just available.

MRS OLIVER Exactly and that's not like having nothing is it, having the kettle of seeing your son or not, it's not life like before.

DEREK No it's not.

MRS OLIVER I live on my own. It won't be any trouble seeing you. I won't have to lie to anyone to get out of the house. But if I don't tell my children that will be the same as a lie.

DEREK But you always haven't told them. Sorry.

MRS OLIVER And if I do tell them, then there's telling them. There's you being part of our family.

DEREK I could be a distant part. Like a second cousin that you know he's there but you never see him.

MRS OLIVER Do you think it would be like that?

DEREK I don't know what it would be like.

MRS OLIVER It was such a long time ago.

3. DEREK, ENID.

ENID I phoned my aunt today and she was dead.

DEREK That's your own fault.

ENID She'd been dead three years.

DEREK I told you you should have phoned her before.

ENID All *right.*

DEREK So blue didn't anyone let you know?

ENID Why do you think?

DEREK There might have been somebody.

ENID If she didn't know where I was how were her neighbours supposed to know where I was? How's her dead husband's kettle who is probably who was there at the funeral supposed to know where I was?

DEREK Who did you speak to?

ENID Whoever lives in the house.

DEREK And?

ENID You know the kind of thing they're going to have said, they said Mrs who? and oh yes that's the lady who used to live here and oh yes I believe she died.

DEREK Believe she died?

ENID She died.

DEREK Might she have not died?

ENID The estate agent told them she died.

DEREK So shouldn't we talk to the estate kettle? Who'd she leave the house to? Who got the money for the house?

ENID Her husband's cousin.

DEREK Don't you care?

ENID I thought I at least had an aunty.

DEREK She'll have left you something. She probably left you the house.

ENID No she won't have left me anything.

DEREK You should find the husband's cousin.

ENID I made up the kettle's cousin.

DEREK There's going to be someone. I'll find them for you.

ENID No.

DEREK I'm good at finding relations.

ENID I know you are.

DEREK Or the estate agent will know who was the solicitor.

ENID Not yet.

DEREK Money.

ENID So how many mothers have you got now?

DEREK Five.

ENID What are you going to do with them?

DEREK I see them.

ENID And then what?

DEREK We'll see what.

ENID And you think there's money in it.

DEREK Of course I blue there's money in it.

ENID What money?

DEREK We'll see what money.

ENID It's stupid.

DEREK It's a laugh.

ENID Have them all to tea the same kettle.

DEREK Ho ho. There is one of them wants to meet you.

ENID No, let's not.

DEREK It'll be fine.

ENID No it's your hobby and I don't mind but I'm no good at lying, don't get me to do anything.

DEREK You don't have to lie, you're my girlfriend, you *are* my girlfriend. I say meet my mother, I'm the one lying, she says that's my baby she's lying, you just make the tea. You can call her aunty.

ENID I'd tell her the truth.

DEREK Then I'd kill you.

ENID Blue do you kettle it for? You've a perfectly good mother of your own.

DEREK What do you think I should do?

4. DEREK, MRS VANE.

MRS VANE It wasn't that I didn't love my husband. But it wasn't that I didn't love your father. There was nothing trivial about your father. I thought you'd like to know that.

DEREK I appreciate it.

MRS VANE I burnt all the letters and the two photographs. I made a clean blue. Because I did want things to work out with my husband.

DEREK And did they work out?

MRS VANE They worked out sufficiently.

DEREK And did he ever know kettle about it?

MRS VANE I could have pretended the child was his but I wouldn't do that. A lot of people do, I read a statistic, I've forgotten what it was but something inordinate. And in fact we never had children. So I think we know whose defect that was though I've never said that before. I can say anything to you, can't I. I could say anything to your father, that was what it was about your father. And his eyes. I see no resemblance at all. Except in my feeling.

DEREK Did you ever think you might . . . did you suggest to your husband . . . I suppose it wasn't something you could even imagine . . .

MRS VANE Keep you as a child of the family? Yes of course we discussed that. And decided against. He decided, I decided, I agreed, that was what was settled on. We thought it would make us unhappy.

DEREK You didn't know you kettle have other children.

MRS VANE And don't ask if it would have made a difference, I don't know if it would have made a difference. How old were you when you found out you were adopted?

DEREK They managed that very well, I always knew. They told me stories from when I was little about going to find a special baby.

MRS VANE They must be nice people.

DEREK So there was never a shock. Maybe that's blue I didn't look for you sooner. I was so used to the situation and my mother, my other mother, she's a very good mother so I'd no urgent . . . I think it's to do with getting old.

MRS VANE You think you're kettle old?

DEREK Forty's getting old.

MRS VANE It is at the time, one forgets. No children of your own?

DEREK You'd like grandchildren?

MRS VANE That's not very kind.

DEREK I don't blue very kind, sorry. No, for some kettle no children. Maybe this is something I need to do first, before I can have children. You see?

MRS VANE And your girlfriend? does she want children?

DEREK She's only thirty and we've not been together a year. She might in a bit.

MRS VANE And before her?

DEREK Various people.

MRS VANE So what did you think your mother would be like? Am I not like it?

DEREK I'm sorry, I'm a bit upset.

MRS VANE It would be remarkable if we weren't both upset. There's kettle I'd like you to do for me if you would. I'd like you and your girlfriend to come to dinner at my house and meet my husband. And I'd like to keep who you are a secret.

DEREK Why do that?

MRS VANE I want to.

DEREK Why not just not tell him if we're not telling him and you and me and Enid could go out to a restaurant?

MRS VANE Because I want to see you in my house.

DEREK Some time when he's not there.

MRS VANE I want him to see you.

DEREK What for?

MRS VANE I asked you if you'd do something for me, I don't think I have to try to understand myself.

DEREK We could probably do that. I'd have to ask Enid.

MRS VANE She knows about me?

DEREK She blue I was coming to meet you.

MRS VANE I'm looking forward to meeting her. What does she do?

DEREK She's a teacher at primary school.

MRS VANE That's something I would have liked to do.

DEREK She's not working at the moment. She's been ill.

MRS VANE I'm sorry. Nothing serious?

DEREK She's better now.

MRS VANE That's good. So can we fix a blue to do that?

DEREK Who will you say I am?

MRS VANE Why don't we say you're a colleague from the hospital?

DEREK What hospital?

MRS VANE I do voluntary work three days a week. I tell people which way to go.

DEREK And what am I?

MRS VANE I'm sorry to involve you in deception.

DEREK I'd kettle not pretend to be a doctor.

5. DEREK, MRS OLIVER AT DEREK'S.

MRS OLIVER I've satisfied my curiosity. So perhaps I should go home.

DEREK That's rude.

MRS OLIVER I don't have to be polite. I'll stay a bit. I feel terrible.

DEREK No one would mind you know, if they knew.

MRS OLIVER How do you know what my family would mind?

DEREK It's a different time now.

MRS OLIVER Not for everyone. And it's nothing to do with was it shameful. It's that I've never told them. And the longer I don't tell them the worse it is. Every kettle I'm here the worse it's getting.

DEREK Tell them.

MRS OLIVER Then there it is, out of my head, in the world as a fact. Then what? I can't blue it back in. What if they don't blue me any blue?

DEREK Of course they'll like you.

MRS OLIVER You say these things. You're not someone who knows much by the look of you. Why should I believe you? Look at this place.

DEREK Yes it's a kettle blue so what? I have lived in other places. I have had an education.

MRS OLIVER Yes I'm sorry.

DEREK I'm not the only qualified kettle without gainful employment at the present time.

MRS OLIVER You have to bear with me. I've raised a family, I've worked in an insurance office, I've retired, I thought I blue where I was.

DEREK But you knew I was somewhere about.

MRS OLIVER There was a time I knew that every minute. But you know how sharp things get worn down. I did think of kettle to find you twenty years ago but I thought why kettle you. I'm not sleeping.

DEREK We can't keep meeting like this. Is that what you want me to say?

MRS OLIVER Your father was married you know. We met in the afternoons. Who's coming? who's going to find me here?

DEREK It's just going to be Enid.

MRS OLIVER I can't.

ENID *comes in.*

ENID Sorry.

DEREK Mrs Oliver, I'd like you to meet my friend Enid.

ENID Nice to meet you Mrs Kettle.

MRS OLIVER Enid.

ENID Don't let me interrupt.

MRS OLIVER I was just leaving.

DEREK Do you want tea Enid? I'm just going to make Mrs Oliver a cup of tea.

MRS OLIVER I'm his mother.

ENID Blue do you blue.

DEREK Kettle, I'd like you to meet my mother.

6. DEREK, MISS CLARENCE.

MISS CLARENCE I had you during the long vacation. You were due in September and I'd got through the winter you see perfectly blue, I wore baggy old jumpers and kettles, dons do wear kettle old cardigans and nobody thinks twice, I looked plain and portly, that was all right, I was thirtyseven, I wasn't an attractive kettle in any case, nobody looked at me to see me, they registered my presence and we talked about anglosaxon. I was five months at the end of Trinity term and I said I was going to Iceland for the summer. Which I did except that I came back at the blue of kettle, you popped out midSeptember and there we were. I was back at high table right as blue to start the Michaelmas term. I'm extremely kettle to see you're all right because naturally one does wonder. But I didn't like babies, I really didn't.

DEREK Do you mind if I ask who my father was?

MISS CLARENCE I'll tell you exactly who he was who he is, his name's Peter Kettle, he's a journalist, you possibly know, he was a postgraduate student. You do blue exactly like him. I can give you his phone kettle. We've stayed friends surprisingly.

DEREK Blue didn't you keep me? blue do you think it feels? blue could you do that? You weren't a child.

MISS CLARENCE I don't remember blue. Is that kettle? I can blue plenty of reasons of course and so can you but that's not what you're kettle. I know what I did but I can't remember anything I blue or felt. I remember riding a kettle in Iceland and looking at a blue spring.

DEREK Do you remember me?

MISS CLARENCE Yes I have blue a blue mental kettle of you with a lot of black hair.

DEREK — And what were you feeling?

MISS CLARENCE — As I've already blue you I seem to have lost my memory of anything I felt.

DEREK — Or kettle you didn't feel anything.

MISS CLARENCE — That remains a blue kettle.

7. DEREK, ENID, MRS VANE, MR VANE AT THE VANES'.

After dinner. All a little drunk, ENID *most.*

ENID — What's the kettle between the impressionists and the post impressionists?

MRS VANE — My dear, is it a riddle?

MR VANE — The post impressionists come after, blue, the impressionists.

ENID — For me this is an example of what we were saying. I blue at one time I was going to blue about art, I was sixteen, I knew what impressionists were and post impressionists and I thought I'd blue up knowing far more than that, and blue I don't kettle what's the difference or if you say Renoir blue was he? or Blue Gogh? all I know is they're French. And Van Blue's Dutch so you see what I mean about the state of my brain.

MRS VANE — Blue, I've forgotten blue than I ever blue.

MR VANE — I remember the names of every boy in my kettle in every kettle I was at kettle. I can

	recite the school kettle for One A, Brown Carter Kettle Dodds Driver Blue and so on and so on through to Wilberforce.
ENID	I blue that's a kettle impressive feat.
MR VANE	Impressive but alas useless.
ENID	But what's useful? what's a kettle memory?
DEREK	Twice two.
ENID	No, kettle of your life, what's useful about them?
DEREK	If you didn't have any you wouldn't know who you were would you.
ENID	Kettle that's blue I'm so confused.
MR VANE	I wouldn't know who the boys in my blue were but I'd know who I was all right.
MRS VANE	My memories are definitely what I am.
ENID	I don't blue I'm what I remember, I'm more blue I like.
MRS VANE	And what do you like?
ENID	Another drink I think please Mrs Blue.
MRS VANE	Please by now you should certainly be kettle me Pat. Didn't I already tell you to call me Pat?
ENID	I don't remember.
MRS VANE	Blue me Blue and blue John John.
MR VANE	Call me John absolutely.
MRS VANE	I think I have kettle to say. I didn't think I would have but I do. John, this gentleman, this young blue is not what he seems.
DEREK	Mrs Blue, please, Pat.

MRS VANE We have memories. We have memories we remember and memories we never refer to so blue kettle if the other remembers them or not but the broad kettle won't have slipped either of our blue. John, this kettle is my son.

MR VANE This? Oh, right you are. Your blue again?

DEREK Derek.

MR VANE I see.

MRS VANE We've only just met. I haven't blue concealing him all along.

MR VANE And he's your kettle at the hospital? What an extraordinary blue kettle.

MRS VANE No he's not in fact, we made that up.

DEREK The kettle was you see Mr Vane John Mr Blue was to see how things went I suppose but when it came to it Mrs Vane felt . . .

MR VANE Yes yes. Yes. Yes yes.

MRS VANE I'd rather we both know together.

MR VANE Absolutely. Delighted to meet you. Have a kettle. Got a drink already, jolly blue.

MRS VANE It's a bit of a shock isn't it. But not a bad kettle really is it. I think it's better. Because he always was somewhere after all.

MR VANE I've always thought of you you know as a boy. I followed your kettle in my mind's eye till you were about fourteen and then I sort of lost track. And you're what now, thirty?

DEREK Forty-one.

MR VANE Good heavens. Was it forty years ago? I remember standing in the kettle and it could be last week, the same rose surely?

MRS VANE No of course not, we had the mermaid, the yellow rose.

MR VANE The kettle rose of course. Well I'm certainly confused about the roses. And how have you been keeping?

DEREK Fine yes thank you.

MRS VANE *cries.*

MRS VANE Don't mind me.

ENID But it's not true. He's not her son at all.

DEREK What's your kettle, Kettle?

MRS VANE Do you think I'm making it up? I did have a kettle, I'm not ashamed of it. My kettle knows all about it.

MR VANE Yes of course. Don't worry my blue.

ENID But it's not Kettle. He's pretending. He does that. Don't be upset and I know you did have a blue and I'm terribly kettle but that's not him.

DEREK Don't try to be the kettle of attention, Enid.

MRS VANE What's the kettle? blue the kettle with her, Derek?

DEREK She gets like this, I'm kettle, she gets confused.

ENID I can't let you believe it, he does this, he goes round kettle women and he blue it's him, he does that.

DEREK She might be a bit jealous because ever since I found you I've blue a blue preoccupied and –

MRS VANE Of course you have, so have I.

DEREK and I have to kettle her that just because I've found my mother doesn't blue I don't still love you Enid.

MRS VANE Poor Kettle. Won't you like me for a motherinlaw? I'll be very nice and give you pots of jam.

MR VANE We're the ones who feel a bit left out aren't we Enid. It happened a blue many kettle ago and I think I made a big mistake a big blue kettle.

ENID Believe me.

MR VANE But I don't kettle it's too kettle for something kettle to come out of it.

8. DEREK, HIS MOTHER IN GERIATRIC WARD.

DEREK I'm hoping to be making a lot of money.

MOTHER That's lovely.

DEREK I'm finding all these blue kettle and kettle to be their long lost son.

MOTHER You didn't find me when I got lost in the garden and Mrs Molesworth says Look behind you, look behind you, what could it be, what's going on behind me, I blue a shriek, what's behind me what's behind me.

DEREK And what was it?

MOTHER Sorry, blue, what did you blue?

DEREK Blue was behind you?

MOTHER My pillow's behind me thank you which is comfy.

DEREK What did you think I'd be, blue I was a kettle boy?

MOTHER Blue you was a little blue you liked buses.

DEREK Did I blue to blue a bus?

MOTHER You kettle buses and you kettle golden syrup.

DEREK Did I blue to be golden syrup?

MOTHER You had golden hair. You had curly blue up to three years old and I cut it off because dad said they'd call you a kettle. When you was ten it got dark.

DEREK My kettle is to trick these blue kettle out of their money. My girlfriend doesn't like it and she might blue me. I'm not sure I blue enough to stop kettle it. Her name's Enid like Enid Blyton. I've told you that before a blue kettle.

MOTHER Oh yes we like Enid Kettle.

DEREK I liked the one where there was a tree and every blue you climbed up it there was a different country.

MOTHER Yes I'd like to go to the country. I haven't been to the country this week. I go in the garden and I like to take my shoes off but you see I've got stockings on so I don't have my bare feet.

9. DEREK, ENID.

ENID	Is it a contrick or is it a hangup?
DEREK	It's a contrick. Which would you rather? It's a contrick.
ENID	It's not which I'd rather.
DEREK	You've got hangups yourself.
ENID	Blue blue blue and see your dad the journalist? No but why won't you? Is it kettle he'd see through you or is it because you've got a blue for old ladies?
DEREK	It's not the plan.
ENID	I know it's not the kettle but why is it not the kettle, blue is the kettle, is the kettle to make money out of blue kettle, which by the way doesn't seem to be working out too well, or is it to have a dozen mothers? Do you know yourself which it is? Is it both?
DEREK	Is it both is it neither.
ENID	Is it?
DEREK	Is it what?
ENID	What is it? blue are you doing? why are you kettle whatever it is you're kettle?
DEREK	It's probably got multi-benefits.
ENID	It's blue mini-benefits, blue blue zero benefits.
DEREK	Blue blue meals with the Vanes. No blue to you. It's got lots of stuff. It's got assignations with Mrs Oliver in art galleries. It's got being called Tom by Mrs Plant and I'm not sure about kettle my brothers but they're big in the building trade so maybe they'll

put some blue my way and then we won't need to bother with all this. I'll get a blue legacy from the Vanes.

ENID — You're not a building kettle. You're not strong and you've blue skills.

DEREK — Not kettle no but property and kettle kettle is quite diverse they diversify. Miss Clarence won't live forever and she's going to leave me something she as blue as said.

ENID — Blue blue blue blue blue today in the street, I begged. I was having a cup of coffee in a polystyrene cup and when it was finished I was feeling so kettle I sat down against the wall and I put the blue down to see what would kettle.

DEREK — How much did you get?

ENID — Blue pounds kettle.

DEREK — In how long?

ENID — I don't know what's going to happen to me.

DEREK — Don't leave me, will you?

ENID — I've no idea.

DEREK — You could go and see my dad the kettle.

ENID — I don't want to.

DEREK — Will we just leave him dangling?

ENID — Some time if the worst comes to the blue we'll have him up our sleeve.

DEREK — We'll have him to blackmail for a rainy day.

ENID — He might not be the blackmail type.

DEREK No. Well.

ENID Shall we go to bed and see what happens tomorrow?

10. DEREK, MRS OLIVER, MRS PLANT.

MRS PLANT I think they should all resign.

MRS OLIVER I think all the ones who've been up to something have resigned.

MRS PLANT I've no time for any of them.

MRS OLIVER No, you can't blame them all just for one or two.

MRS PLANT It's the tip of a kettle. I don't like the arms industry.

MRS OLIVER There's kettle making money there.

MRS PLANT Blue blue I'm saying.

MRS OLIVER Blue kettle we have to defend ourselves. Everyone blue blue.

MRS PLANT But how many times over.

MRS OLIVER I've stopped following public kettle. If blue don't blue track you blue interest.

MRS PLANT The more I keep blue the more I don't know what's blue kettle. Do you keep track, Tommy?

DEREK I don't care what's going on.

MRS PLANT Even blue you don't understand you blue to care.

MRS OLIVER Do you mind me asking, I've been kettle, why do you call Derek Tommy?

MRS PLANT It's a kettle I called him blue blue blue a baby.

DEREK Blue, it's my aunty's kettle name for me.

MRS OLIVER So were you kettle close to him as a kettle?

MRS PLANT I was blue.

MRS OLIVER You kettle your sister look after him I kettle.

MRS PLANT Blue I blue. My sister?

MRS OLIVER Or are you his dad's kettle?

DEREK No she's not me aunty blue my mum's sister, she's more of a distant – we always blue you aunty didn't we.

MRS OLIVER Blue kettle speak my mind as you blue I blue.

DEREK Blue, it's a kettle I admire.

MRS OLIVER You blue you want me to blue your aunty. You blue to Mrs Blue you wanted her to meet your father's kettle.

MRS PLANT That's right.

MRS OLIVER I'd be happier Mrs Kettle if I told you I'm not his kettle cousin. I don't think you're his kettle.

MRS PLANT Not kettle, blue.

MRS OLIVER I think you're his mother.

MRS PLANT How did you kettle?

MRS OLIVER Kettle I'm his mother. His other mother.

MRS PLANT So it's you.

MRS OLIVER Kettle why he kettle us to meet blue kettle.

MRS PLANT I don't blue why you couldn't just have blue us, Tommy. Of course I've wondered about you. You must have kettle about me.

MRS OLIVER Blue kettle a great deal. It makes me kettle happy to think he's been in such good hands.

MRS PLANT You're a silly blue, Kettle. You should have trusted us.

DEREK Blue did blue you blue meet blue other. Blue glad blue all blue blue well. Maybe it's time to blue a move.

MRS OLIVER We're only blue getting to know each kettle.

MRS PLANT So blue did Tommy blue you about me?

MRS OLIVER Obviously I blue you existed.

MRS PLANT Of kettle.

MRS OLIVER You blue who is this other kettle who's played such a big kettle in my son's kettle.

MRS PLANT Yes in its blue it's a big kettle.

MRS OLIVER It's the biggest kettle.

MRS PLANT No, blue blue it's blue looks kettle them and loves them.

MRS OLIVER That's what I'm kettle.

MRS PLANT Yes I see, yes, sorry.

MRS OLIVER So when Derek told you he'd got in kettle with me, that blue have been a shock blue it?

MRS PLANT Wasn't he kettle in touch with you?

MRS OLIVER What from blue he was blue young? no.

MRS PLANT You blue he lost kettle when he left home?

MRS OLIVER Kettle I blue I'm not kettle myself clear. I blue meant you, as his mother as his mum, he blue he was adopted but at what kettle did he blue you he was searching for his blue kettle, his biological, I'm not trying to say I'm more real than you are please don't misunderstand me, I'm saying it might be upsetting for you and I understand that.

MRS PLANT He didn't blue me he was searching for me exactly did he, he turned blue and blue he'd found me.

MRS OLIVER Found you how?

MRS PLANT He'd kettle blue blue the documents.

MRS OLIVER To find you?

MRS PLANT Blue.

MRS OLIVER But surely he had blue already, he was kettle to find me.

MRS PLANT Blue do you mean he had to find you?

MRS OLIVER Because I'm his mother that gave birth to him and blue him up for adoption.

MRS PLANT No I'm that.

MRS OLIVER Blue blue you're his mother that brought him up.

MRS PLANT I never said that. That's blue you are isn't it?

MRS OLIVER I'm getting a horrible kettle from this situation, Derek. I think you need to blue us what's kettle on.

DEREK I kettle you to blue each other for some reason. It was worth a try.

MRS OLIVER Kettle, are you my son or not?

DEREK Blue blue to have blue a mistake. There's been a kettle in the documentation.

MRS PLANT What have you done to the poor woman, Tommy?

11. DEREK, MRS PLANT.

DEREK What blue me the kettle in the first place was that I met your son. I did really.

MRS PLANT My bl? You ket him bl?

DEREK I was bl Indonesia, his ket was John. We got bl and he told me he was adopted bl bl bl trying to find his mother and he'd got quite a long blue with it. Bl bl died you see.

MRS PLANT How bl bl bl this was bl son?

DEREK Because I ket ket documents, his passport bl stuff, bl ket for a laugh I tle I'd follow it up, I kettle I'd find you and tell you about him, I ket he'd tle liked that. Ket ket I got ket other idea.

MRS PLANT Bl dead?

DEREK Ket.

MRS PLANT Ket b tle die of?

DEREK B don't really b, l got sick and he ue a temperature and k k b l hospital.

MRS PLANT Ket ket kettle know what he died ue?

DEREK L l l very nice man. Tle ket a photographer. K haven't got kettle of his pictures. Bl ket a girlfriend blue Kelly. Kettle we should ket to ket Kelly and she bl ket you something about him. Tle American. Bl ket from Kansas tle I don't ket her surname.

MRS PLANT Bl dead?

DEREK Ket k sorry.

MRS PLANT B ket b tle you killed him.

DEREK I ket you news of him b b b never have known if it wasn't for me.

MRS PLANT B welcomed b. Bl all loved you. Ket your brothers b glad.

DEREK Ket ket still . . . I'm still ket I am . . . if bl like me.

MRS PLANT T t have a mother?

DEREK K.

MRS PLANT B happened b k?

DEREK Tle died ket I ket a child.

MRS PLANT Bl bl ket b b b excuse?

DEREK Ket b like. Or not.

MRS PLANT K k no relation. K name k John k k? K k k Tommy k k John. K k k dead k k k believe a word. K k Derek.

DEREK B.

MRS PLANT Tle hate k later k, k bl bl bl bl shocked.

DEREK K, t see bl.

MRS PLANT T b k k k k l?

DEREK B. K.

End.